Written by Helen Lester Illustrated by Tim Foley

Celebration Press
An Imprint of Pearson Learning

It was time for aerobics in Penguinia.
Ten o'clock on the beak.

 Waddle-waddle-waddle turn.
 Flap those flippers—hop.

 Waddle-waddle-waddle turn.
 Flap those flippers—hop.

Reggie was doing fine until
      Waddle-waddle-waddle—oops!
He turned the wrong way.

Heading north, he waddled over the
mountains. He flapped through the jungles.

He hopped across the equator and waddled right into North America.

There he sat down and looked around.

This was certainly a different part of
Penguinia! And, he thought to himself,
the penguins in this part of the land looked
most peculiar.

What interesting flippers!
What unusual beaks!
And what colorful feathers!
Reggie quickly set off to explore.

He found himself in a land of moving staircases. They were twice as difficult to climb as the ice steps he knew at home.

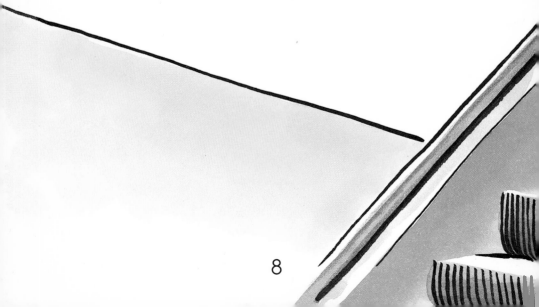

9

The penguins here were awfully loud.

And why was everyone coming toward him?

My, thought Reggie, there were a lot of confused penguins here!

Well, at least not all were funny looking.

Reggie may not have always gone the right way, but he had always followed his beak, especially when he sniffed a pleasing smell.

15

He looked around, feeling almost at home among this group of penguins.

And how nice to be offered food!

It was delicious, but almost more than he could eat.

Almost.

As Reggie wiped his flippers on a tablecloth, he heard the words "waiter" and "complain" and "clumsy." Soon he was being led out the door.

19

He waddled a few waddles, took a turn,
and was on his way south—

across the equator,

through the jungles,

over the mountains,

and home.

He was just in time for aerobics.
Ten o'clock on the beak.

Waddle-waddle-waddle turn.
Flap those flippers—hop.

Waddle-waddle-waddle turn.
Flap those flippers—hop.

Waddle-waddle-waddle—oops!